WHAT YOU NEED TO KNOW BEFORE YOU SHELL OUT $10,000 (OR MORE) ON A PATENT

Doctor In Charge Of Patent Funding At Major University Reveals How She Decides Which Ideas Are Worth Protecting...And Which Ones NEVER Make The Cut!

by Rob Gramer

Warning-Disclaimer: I wrote this report to provide information in regard to the subject matter covered. It is offered with the understanding that the publisher and the author are not liable for the misconception or misuse of the information provided.

Every effort has been made to make this report as complete and accurate as possible. The purpose of this report is to educate. The author and the publisher shall have neither liability nor responsibility to any person or entity with respect to any loss, damage, or injury caused or alleged to be caused directly or indirectly by the information contained in this report. No offer of investment is being made. The information presented herein is in no way intended as a substitute for legal counseling.

Go to www.inventionprep.com to learn how to start profiting off your idea in the next 30 days.

2

Inside:

Go to www.inventionprep.com to learn how to start profiting off your idea in the next 30 days.

3

Go to www.inventionprep.com to learn how to
start profiting off your idea in the next 30 days.

4

Go to www.inventionprep.com to learn how to start profiting off your idea in the next 30 days.

5

Introduction

This book is going to present to you a very different take on patenting ideas. In fact, you're going to hear something pretty much NO patent attorney with their own law firm will ever tell you.

The goal of this book is simple.

To give you the information to determine if your idea - the idea that will most likely cost $10,000 or more to patent - is worth investing in.

Because, ultimately, if you spend $10,000 or more on a patent...you want to make that money back (and then some), right?

You want that $10,000 to turn into $20,000...$100,000 ...$1 million or more.

But Most People Fail!

Well, I'm here to tell you, that doesn't always happen.

This book will explain why.

Go to www.inventionprep.com to learn how to start profiting off your idea in the next 30 days.

And will give you a few simple, straightforward tactics for turning a profit on your idea inside of the first 30 days.

Now, I have to warn you. This is much different than what you'll usually hear about patents and the process of protecting your ideas.

The reason why I say this is because the following pages are based off an interview with someone I call a "patent gatekeeper".

Is Your Idea Worth Patenting?

Her name is Christine Gramer. She is a patent agent and holds her doctorate in chemistry from one of the top 3 universities in the world - the University of California in Berkley.

And she's drafted patents for Eli Lilly, a global pharmaceutical company with sales of $23 billion in 2013.

And she is my sister.

Go to www.inventionprep.com to learn how to start profiting off your idea in the next 30 days.

7

Today, she works at the University of Oregon in their technology development department. There, she reviews all of the ideas the university faculty produces. And she decides whether or not these ideas will or will not receive university money for patent protection.

That means, she literally looks at hundreds of ideas every year, from a wide variety of different angles...and determines whether or not they are worth it for the university to pursue.

Beware Who You Look to for Advice

I want to make an important point here...this is much different than what most patent attorneys do.

I know. I worked at a law firm that specializes in patents for two years.

And let me share with you a dirty little secret...

If you go to a patent attorney to ask about BUSINESS advice, you are asking for trouble.

Go to www.inventionprep.com to learn how to start profiting off your idea in the next 30 days.

8

Patent attorneys are NOT experts in business or marketing.

Think about it...

What do you think a patent attorney does all day?

Do you think they create advertising for new ideas and help bring them to market? Do you think they research the buying behavior of groups of customers? Do you think they scour trade journals to see which products are selling and which aren't?

NOT a Chance!

No, of course not...

I'll tell you what they do.

They talk to inventors.

They get the facts of the invention.

And then they draft the patent application. Or, if they are a bigger firm, they HIRE someone to draft the application and manage the secretaries...patent agents...and engineers that work in the office.

Go to www.inventionprep.com to learn how to start profiting off your idea in the next 30 days.

And guess what?

That has NOTHING to do with marketing or selling the idea.

Yes, they must know the intricacies of patent law and make sure your application is written to get maximum protection.

But sales? Not a chance.

#1 Reason Why Inventors Fail

YET...one of the first questions new inventors had when they visited the firm I worked for was, "Do you think I'll be able to make money with this idea?"

That's like asking a plumber for fashion advice. Unless you want to dress in dirty old overalls...the end result isn't going to be pretty.

You go to patent attorneys for legal advice on protecting your idea. If you ask them business advice...don't be surprised if you end up spending tens of thousands of dollars and have nothing to show for it.

Go to www.inventionprep.com to learn how to start profiting off your idea in the next 30 days.

Which is why I think you'll really enjoy this conversation I had with Christine.

That's because...even though she's studied patent law and drafted tons of patents, she's now on the other side of the fence.

Now, she has to decide if it makes FINANCIAL SENSE for the university to invest in patenting ideas the university faculty produce.

She has to decide if there is...

- A commercial application for the idea. If they patent it, can the faculty start a business and sell aspects of the idea (of which the university takes a percentage)?
- A licensing aspect of the idea. Is this something the university can license out for a profit?
- A necessary protection aspect so the faculty can continue research. Remember, much university research is supplied by government grants or private funding. Sometimes a patent is necessary so the faculty can continue

Go to www.inventionprep.com to learn how to start profiting off your idea in the next 30 days.

11

research (and continue receiving money from outside sources).

In essence, she has to decide if the patent is financially viable!

And so should you, before you hand over tens of thousands of dollars to patent attorney.

Which is why I think you'll find the rest of the information in this book so valuable. Without further ado, let's begin...

Go to www.inventionprep.com to learn how to start profiting off your idea in the next 30 days.

12

Rob: So to start off this interview, can you give us your big picture background, kind of where you came from, how you got into this field, what your degrees are, thinks like that?

What's your back story?

Christine: So I have PHD in Chemistry from UC Berkley. After graduate school I worked for a small to medium size Biotech company in their patent department.

I was interested more in intellectual property as I got first into my graduate career and I was fortunate enough to get this job, preparing patent applications, writing patent applications, doing background research, prior art searches for this company.

I was there for a year and half and after that moved to the University of

Go to www.inventionprep.com to learn how to start profiting off your idea in the next 30 days.

13

Oregon. Now I have a position in our office.

Many universities call it technology transfer. Our office is called innovation partnership services. We manage any sort of innovation that comes out of university research that could be transferred into the private sector.

So that might mean through a license agreement or through an existing company or could mean that we have focusing on our campus and want to form a startup company.

We also handle a lot of other, you know, consulting with folks on issues of intellectual property and how to manage it...whether it's publication, their freedom to operate or trademarks, copyright issues as well as patent issues for them.

Go to www.inventionprep.com to learn how to start profiting off your idea in the next 30 days.

14

And I'm also a patent agent and I have been at this job for almost 11 years now.

Rob: So basically, faculty or anybody at the college there, as they are doing research and, if they come up with an idea they can bring it to your department and will find out whether or not this is something that...

A. qualifies for patent, or...

B. doesn't qualify for a patent.

And then you tell them whether or not this is something that they can go ahead and go through the process and get protection for?

Christine: Yeah generally and of course because we are a large campus we get people with all different types of interest and experience with, you know forming a company or you know, forming doing something with the business.

Go to www.inventionprep.com to learn how to start profiting off your idea in the next 30 days.

15

Sometimes people come to us because they think like, wow, this seems like to be really useful and somebody could do something good with it.

So they themselves are not really interested in pursuing, you know the commercial side of that innovation.

They just might want to partner with somebody or have some advice on that. And we also have folks on campus who are not like on the research side of thing but have developed, you know, maybe, a mobile app or something in the area of software where they may or may not think about patenting but still think about commercialization and protecting intellectual property.

So for us one of the big things to evaluate is once somebody brings technology to us, the best type of position that we could possibly have at

Go to www.inventionprep.com to learn how to start profiting off your idea in the next 30 days.

16

university is if it's a platform
technology.

So that would mean something that's
really like early stage ground breaking
and is the basis of a lot of other
development.

This is a little bit different than
like what an independent inventor might
do.

They might have something more like a
specific product in line and so when
they want to file a patent application
they are going to define their claims
based on what they think the commercial
embodiment of what the invention is
going to be. Whereas when faculty comes
to us, they are at the beginning stages
of the research process, they have
discovered something new maybe some
chemical compositions that you know,
you could make thousands of if not
millions of different derivatives.

Go to www.inventionprep.com to learn how to
start profiting off your idea in the next 30 days.

17

The challenge for us is, first of all, is filling a patent application early enough that we stay out ahead of their publication schedule.

(**Rob's Note**: You have to file a patent before you publicly disclose your idea. And since faculty at colleges frequently publish papers on their research, the patent team must make sure to submit an application for a patent before these papers are published.)

And that means sometimes we don't have the idea fully enabled like they haven't got all the different compounds or all the different testing but they are going to give a presentation at a conference somewhere so we have to file the patent application before they talk about it publicly.

And then the other choice for us is that because patents can be expensive,

Go to www.inventionprep.com to learn how to start profiting off your idea in the next 30 days.

18

even though platform technology keeps us in the best position it also mean we have to consider how many patents to apply for. Because it could be that there would be like maybe 8 or 10 different patents that could come out of one idea.

You can't afford to do all of them so we are kind of on the clock right away...at the early stages of research for either getting entrepreneurs in place or doing some of the due diligent or market research to figure out is this a viable company.

The difference within independent venture being that they can keep their ideas secret for longer and then have time to kind of do some of the market research and refine their idea and therefore refine their patent application for maybe just to only file a couple of patent application on a more specific area.

Go to www.inventionprep.com to learn how to start profiting off your idea in the next 30 days.

19

Rob: Hmm, that's interesting.

Okay and so we talked about this before and you know my background, I worked for a law firm before. I worked for a patent attorney. And that's a business, they made money by charging people to do patent searches and through patent applications whereas you do sort of on the other side.

Your job is to basically say no. To tell all of these researchers and faculty that the university is not going to spend money on doing this application because of xyz.

So I think that's really interesting because a lot of people don't understand that patent attorney's are businessmen.

They get paid by charging people to do stuff which isn't always in the best interest of the inventor. Because it

Go to www.inventionprep.com to learn how to start profiting off your idea in the next 30 days.

20

doesn't always makes sense to patent their idea.

So with that in mind, when you are evaluating an idea that somebody brings to you, what are some of the thoughts that are going through your head, what are some of the questions that you are asking about it to see whether or not it makes the cut?

Christine: Yeah, so we have a few different motivations here as well.

So for instance if we know somebody is working in a really crowded field and we worry about freedom to operate or we were worried that their might be somebody else pursuing commercial interest.

They are trying to submit a patent application for a faculty simply because the university is protecting

Go to www.inventionprep.com to learn how to
start profiting off your idea in the next 30 days.

21

faculty members right to go continue working in that area.

Because a patent can give you the right to exclude somebody else, we wouldn't want our faculty member to be excluded from doing an area of research that they were trying to pursue because one of their competitors would looking at some commercial opportunities and maybe licensing to a private company.

So we definitely have some interest in some different types of motivation for patenting and it's not always just a straight line.

I mean a lot of time, we will kind of go on answers or best assumption and maybe we file a provisional patent application and give ourselves time to sort of qualify those leads, to make the phone calls to see who might be interested, to see how that project develops.

Go to www.inventionprep.com to learn how to start profiting off your idea in the next 30 days.

22

And then a provisional patent expires in one year, and so at that one year point hopefully we've gathered enough market information at that point to know whether or not, you know this is something we are just going to abandon or we are going to go ahead and file full patent application.

Rob: So you're saying a patent is an asset.

So it's not, once you patent something now, there's 15 different ways you can use it like you mentioned, you know, for individual inventors, they are gonna want to probably sell the idea, license the idea or actually sell the product.

Whereas what you are saying is some of the researchers, they want to protect it so they can actually continue doing research in that field rather than simply selling a product.

Go to www.inventionprep.com to learn how to start profiting off your idea in the next 30 days.

23

So that's something that, I didn't know that was the way they did it.

When somebody brings an idea to you, what kind of questions do you ask, how do you evaluate whether or not this is something that is really worth moving forward on and actually filing the full provisional patent or non provisional patent application on it.

Christine: Yeah, so, there's a lot of different factors you can evaluate on.

First of all do prior art searches. You might want to poke around and see what prior art is out there.

(**Rob's Notes:** Prior Art refers to any other products, inventions, or patents that are similar to the idea...that would prevent you from securing patent protection...or - in some cases - would indicate you are infringing against someone else's patent).

Go to www.inventionprep.com to learn how to start profiting off your idea in the next 30 days.

24

You can do this by using google to search for companies that might be in that area. Or you know you can go on google patents and search other patents online...definitely do a lot of searching to understand what else might be out there.

The other question of course is always the market. Because there are many times - and even with start-up companies - when you may want to license out a patent (or license someone else's patent).

Rob: So again getting back to this idea that a patent is an asset. That this is something you can buy, rent, or sell like any other asset?

Christine: Yes.

On the other hand we definitely have people come to us with little specific narrow ideas and they are folks who are

Go to www.inventionprep.com to learn how to start profiting off your idea in the next 30 days.

25

very commercially minded and sort of entrepreneurially motivated.

In those cases, even though it seems like something small you might want to contact a university and see if there is someone there who can help you pursue it.

Somebody there may wants to take it out to the marketplace and develop that further.

We have contacts in the community with other entrepenurs, so we can put people in contact with other people who can help them...research the product, research the market, provide business support. Things of that nature.

Rob: Got it.

So you are saying that you are in the University of Oregon, but you are also mentioning that most big universities

Go to www.inventionprep.com to learn how to
start profiting off your idea in the next 30 days.

26

have these different departments within them.

So you are saying that people outside of the university will also come to you and say hey listen this is my idea, what could we do with it, who do you know could help, those sort of things...and perhaps you put them contact with people that you know who can help them out with that?

Christine: We have a strong network and we know lot of the folks in the business community. For example, we work closely with the Chamber of Commerce.

There are number of people in town, who had or have successful companies, so they have backgrounds in different areas and even if they are not bringing in technology to us they might come over and meet us.

Go to www.inventionprep.com to learn how to start profiting off your idea in the next 30 days.

27

Or they might be somebody who we know, who knows a specific technology...and we can ask them if they are interested in this area...would you be interested in "such and such" faculty member and you know, forming a LLC or forming a company?

So I think a big part of this, especially in the small community that we are in is networking within the local business community and entrepreneurs in town.

But we actually really don't take in outside inventors. I can't think of a single example where we've really brought in technology from outside that somebody has brought too.

If I get a call from somebody I will consult, I will give them advice and kinda tell them what they are up against and point them in the right direction but we don't bring that

Go to www.inventionprep.com to learn how to start profiting off your idea in the next 30 days.

28

technology into the university and manage it.

Rob: Ok. So that may be a thing somewhere else that could be a resource. An inventor may be able to visit their local university and ask, "do you have a technology department that deals with inventions? Can I talk to somebody there?

That may or may not be an option

Christine: Yeah, right. If somebody calls me, I will say ok, who on campus have you spoken to.

What stage of advise do you need? Are you just kind of curious about being pointed in the right direction and meeting some of the other people? That will help you.

As with a real research project where you need to partner with a faculty member...that gets a little trickier

Go to www.inventionprep.com to learn how to start profiting off your idea in the next 30 days.

29

because that gets into issues of research and you know that's up to the interest levels of that faculty member.

But yeah, we can definitely be a starting point to kind of make introduction and generally give advice.

Yeah, it's a little different than somebody who started off as an established entrepreneur, looking for technology they would like to bring in to the market.

Rob: Yeah, of course.

Okay. So as far as the actual drafting of the patent is concerned, lets say, I am a new inventor and I want to hire an attorney and agent to draft this thing up for me.

And generally what are you looking for the person? Do you want them to just, kind of jot out their idea? Do you want

Go to www.inventionprep.com to learn how to start profiting off your idea in the next 30 days.

30

drawings from them? Do you want prototypes?

What are you looking for before you actually get into the work of putting together the application for the patent?

Christine: So we use our patent attorneys to do all of the drafting for us.

I just don't have the bandwidth and all the time to do that as well as the rest my work.

But based on my previous experience, I would do an interview with the faculty member where I have a number of various questions I ask them.

You know after they told me about the invention itself and I asked them some of the pros and cons and things like that, I'll say have you talked about this to anybody?

Go to www.inventionprep.com to learn how to start profiting off your idea in the next 30 days.

31

Have you publicly disclosed your idea?

What form have you talked to somebody (face to face, given a speech, etc.)?

Have you offered it for sale?

Told it to your family?

Have you gone to any kind of meeting where you have talked about this or published any kind of papers?

Have you put it up on your website?

So anything where you talking not in confidentiality, this can be considered a public disclosure.

In the United States, we have one year grace period from the time you make a public disclosure until you can file a patent application.

Otherwise your own work will be held as prior art against your patent application.

Go to www.inventionprep.com to learn how to start profiting off your idea in the next 30 days.

32

So that's the first think I always ask people, you know, tell me about your previous disclosures that you have done.

Rob: You are talking about one year time frame. Once they say something, they have to file for a patent within on year?

Christine: That's right yeah, the one year if someone they talked about it publicly.

And another thing I ask them about extensively is tell me what other people in this field have done.

You know if you are writing a paper of who you are referencing and then, they usually are only thinking about for the academic literature. And then I have to go in and all work through the patent literature because they don't generally search the patent literature.

Go to www.inventionprep.com to learn how to start profiting off your idea in the next 30 days.

33

I'd do this to make the outside patent council job of preparing the patent application as easy as possible. By doing the information gathering ahead of time.

Rob: Ok. So you are saying that if there's an inventor and they are going to sit down with an attorney or agent or somebody, if they are hiring somebody to draft up their patent for them, it would be a good idea for them to...

...get a good description of what it is that they have, get a good description of how they disclose that either talking to people or putting up a website or so on and so forth and then...

...three, also if they had any sort of research done on competitors or anything else on the market, bringing that as well.

Go to www.inventionprep.com to learn how to start profiting off your idea in the next 30 days.

34

All that ammo for the agent or the attorney will need to draft this application for them.

Christine: Yeah and one of the other good things to do is an outline. List out the advantages or disadvantages.

(**Rob's notes**: advantages of your idea...what benefit it gives to the person using it. Does it save time? Does it save money? Is it easier to use?)

Make a list of how your invention is distinguished from everything else already out there.

So in the patent examination process, there's this idea of anticipation. That means if somebody else has already disclosed or is selling similar products...you are not going to be able to get a patent application to issue.

Go to www.inventionprep.com to learn how to start profiting off your idea in the next 30 days.

35

The other idea - which is really tricky - is this idea of obviousness. That is where you take two things that are out there and combine them and get the result. And that is your product.

If it is really obvious you are going to have a real hard time getting clearance issued to your patent application.

That's because the patent office is going to say, you can't take something out of the public domain that's already out there. Because a patent gives you an exclusive twenty year ownership of your idea, that exclusionary period prevents other people from practicing the invention.

The patent office has a bar that's pretty high. To overcome this obviousness objection, you have to have some sort of extra benefit to doing what it is that you are doing.

Go to www.inventionprep.com to learn how to start profiting off your idea in the next 30 days.

36

Rob: I remember a specific example of this.

I want to say the company was Motorola. Years ago they submitted a patent application of a cell phone combined with a camera and they wanted to patent the idea of a cell phone camera.

When they put the patent through and when it got to the prosecution part, they said no.

The patent office called this obvious. That eventually somebody would combine a phone and a camera and so no, we are not going to give you the patent for a cell phone camera.

And that would have been huge for motorola, because obviously every cell phone now has a camera on it.

So I think that's what you are mentioning is that if somebody has an

Go to www.inventionprep.com to learn how to start profiting off your idea in the next 30 days.

37

idea that's obvious, they are not going to let it go through.

Christine: Right, and obvious has different meanings. People us it colloquially, the word obvious. But it does have a real legal meaning in the patent world. And you have to be careful how you throw that word around in any kind of correspondence with your patent attorney or anybody else.

Rob: So going back to the original question, not only do you want to say here's the idea, here's where I disclose it, here's my competitors but now you also want to say here's why it's different.

Here's how I will distinguish it from anything else out there.

And also here's why it's not an obvious type of thing. Correct?

Go to www.inventionprep.com to learn how to start profiting off your idea in the next 30 days.

38

Christine: Yeah, those are good things to think about and your patent attorney would guide you through sort of the questions you might be thinking about ...especially, the answer to the idea of obviousness.

These are the things to think about ahead of time.

Rob: Ok, anything else that you would want to put together and show the attorney or the agent before you meet them?

Christine: Well, you mentioned a prototype.

You actually don't have to have a prototype to get a patent for something.

You do however have to be able to describe stepwise and accurately how somebody would build that prototype and why it would be expected to work the

Go to www.inventionprep.com to learn how to start profiting off your idea in the next 30 days.

39

way you are telling somebody it would work.

So you don't actually have to build it. But if you have one that's really valuable for few reasons.

First, because it could be that in building it you realize a couple of flaws in the design that needs to be fixed or tinkered with.

If you just had a simple written out description, it might not have really been an operable invention.

So it's not a bad idea to get as far as you can and build in a prototype or different variations on a prototype.

Second, something a lot of inventors don't realize is that their invention is actually a lot bigger than they think it is.

Go to www.inventionprep.com to learn how to start profiting off your idea in the next 30 days.

40

Their prototype might turn out to be one embodiment and their invention might actually be a bigger concept.

And so sometimes building that prototype allows you to see, oh, this feature could operate in three different ways and then your patent attorney will be able to build that type of description into your patent application.

Rob: What you are hitting on is really that some inventors may think their invention has a very narrow focus. But the job of the patent attorney and the patent agent is to really expand that focus as much as possible so that the inventor is getting as much protection as possible for the idea and not just how they are narrowly using it.

Christine: That is exactly correct.

Go to www.inventionprep.com to learn how to start profiting off your idea in the next 30 days.

41

That is exactly the job of your patent attorney to get you the broadest possible coverage that you are legally entitled to.

Rob: Ok, so how about this example...

Let's say there's no such thing as a blimp or a helicopter or an airplane and I have built a blimp...

...I wouldn't want to just patent the concept of a blimp, I would want to patent the concept of a "flying machine".

And try to get as much coverage for any kind of flying machine as it is, not just the original idea, the blimp.

And I think that's very important because, you know, a lot of people when they invent something, if they are not in a different field, they don't know how important it could be and how much more they could get out of it.

Go to www.inventionprep.com to learn how to start profiting off your idea in the next 30 days.

42

Christine: Yeah.

Another thing I think about is whether or not this is an improvement.

This could be a huge problem.

Just because you have a patent that issues to you, doesn't mean that you are not infringing on somebody else's patent.

So the idea is you improve on someone else's patented idea...where you have taken somebody else's work and you have improved on it in a patentable way but the broader patent is still out there.

Even if you work as a better embodiment, you might have to have a cross licensing situation or situation where you would want to license their broader patent.

But of course, there would be a motivation for them to license to you

Go to www.inventionprep.com to learn how to start profiting off your idea in the next 30 days.

43

because you know there might be increased sales based on your patent application.

And so I get more into the question of licensing or how you manage it on a business aspect. But it is important to realize that having a patent doesn't give you the right to practice your invention.

It only gives you the right to exclude other people.

For example, let's say there's a patent for a three legged stool out there, and you come up with the idea of five legged stool because it's more stable, it won't tip over easily.

If that three legged stool patent is written correctly, your five legged stool wouldn't change that three legged stool patent. A five legged stool is

Go to www.inventionprep.com to learn how to start profiting off your idea in the next 30 days.

44

just a three legged stool with two extra legs.

So that's an example where you might need cross licensing to think about, what are the dominating patents that are out there in the field.

Rob: And that's something that would come up hopefully in the patent searches or in the research phase.

Before you actually got the patent, hopefully in this five legged stool case, somebody would find those three legged stool and they would say hey listen, you can still get a patent for five legged stool. Nothing stopping you from doing that.

But, before you go forth and create a five legged stool, you're going to have to get permission from the guy who owns a three legged stool patent.

Christine: That's right.

Go to www.inventionprep.com to learn how to start profiting off your idea in the next 30 days.

45

Rob: This is interesting, okay.

That's really why it's important for somebody to go out there and do the research before they spent say $10,000 on the patent and another $100,000 on prototype.

You really want to get your house in order intellectual property wise before you forward.

Christine: Right, and your patent attorney or patent agent can do patentability analysis for you while they search the prior art and they give you an opinion.

It may give you some strategy that you might use in preparing your own patent application to kind of work around what other folks have done.

And it may give you preview of what a patent examiner may pull up or find relevant. Or maybe simply by disclosing

Go to www.inventionprep.com to learn how to start profiting off your idea in the next 30 days.

46

these other patents that are out there...they'll look at your application and decide, you know, you've done a good enough job working around everything.

Rob: Hmm, that's interesting. Now are you saying that by filing other patents, do your searches at the beginning and then including those references in the actual application itself...you can make the job of the person approving or denying the patent a little bit easier? Is that's what you are alluding to?

Christine: Well, if you are aware of anything that you think is relevant to your invention, you have a duty to disclose it during the patent application process.

There's a form that you fill up, it's called information disclosure, you have a duty to disclose any kind of art that

Go to www.inventionprep.com to learn how to start profiting off your idea in the next 30 days.

47

you have come across that you think is relevant that you want the patent examiner to consider.

And I've actually gotten two different opinions on this. And it depends on who is the patent attorney who is working for you.

Some of them say, if you search the art and you have made your case as to why your invention is different and what else is out there that the patent examiner appreciates this and it could make the job of examining easier.

The other opinion I've got is I never do a prior art search, I prepare the patent application in as broad a way possible way. That way I can leave the job of searching to the patent examiner and I let them tell me what they think is relevant.

Go to www.inventionprep.com to learn how to start profiting off your idea in the next 30 days.

48

So maybe that gets you a broader patent...but it's also maybe a more expensive route to go because the patent might be so broad that patent prosecution takes a long time.

And that brings us to the patent application review process.

Right now, the patent office allows for a review process. If you didn't disclose everything that you know about, you kept some of your findings secret and that's discovered, your patent can simply be held invalid.

So there's actually a legal requirement on the people familiar with the case that they just disclose anything that they know.

Rob: So that brings up a very important point about fees. It's not just for the patent attorney directing the application.

Go to www.inventionprep.com to learn how to start profiting off your idea in the next 30 days.

49

Christine: Once you submit it, and it's reviewed, there's may be more fees involved if you have to go back and forth.

It's almost like an appeals process. So the patent examiner asks you to clarify this...and then you have to hire your patent attorney again to clarify parts of your application.

That's another fee that the inventor will have to shoulder, basically before this patent has approved.

Rob: So everybody listening just to make us abundantly clear, the fee that you pay upfront for the patent application is not it.

You may have other fees on the back end during the approval process and maintenance fees over the course of the years.

Go to www.inventionprep.com to learn how to start profiting off your idea in the next 30 days.

50

Ok, that was a really good point. Anything else do you think is important to this conversation?

Christine: The American Patent Act has been rolled out in stages over the past few years. There have been a lot of major changes to the patent system in the U.S. So people might want to check out the United States Patent and Trademark Office website at www.uspto.gov for more info.

Keep in mind, any articles online may be out of date if the information was published before these new changes rolled out.

Rob: Perfect. Well, do you want to add anything else?

Christine: I think that's a really good starting point, those are good things for people to consider. Good luck.

Go to www.inventionprep.com to learn how to start profiting off your idea in the next 30 days.

51

How do you find a trustworthy patent attorney?

There are a TON of steps involved in making your dream a reality. From patent protection, to design and engineering, to marketing your idea...and much more.

That's where I come in. I help people who have ideas and inventions (just like you) find the right people to help them out.

I can also show you:

- How to save thousands of dollars on legal fees while patenting your invention

- How to find designers and engineers to create your ideas on paper and in real life (from sketches to prototypes, to mass manufacturing) quicker than you ever dreamed possible

- And, how to get all the money you need WITHOUT investors...usually within 30 days (AND you get to keep ALL your equity)

Most people think it takes a major investment of time and money to get their ideas off the ground.

Go to www.inventionprep.com to learn how to start profiting off your idea in the next 30 days.

Now you can start profiting from your ideas and inventions in as little as 30 days.

If you'd like me to help, just send an email to Rob@inventionprep.com and we'll take it from there.

Go to www.inventionprep.com to learn how to start profiting off your idea in the next 30 days.

53

Awesome Free Bonuses!

Visit www.inventionprep.com for free instant access to more free cool stuff like...

- Personal feedback from licensed patent professionals, engineers, and experienced marketers on how to protect, create, and sell your idea.
- How to save thousands on legal fees to protect your idea
- Quickly and cheaply create prototypes and final products (in days instead of weeks or months)
- Profit from your idea as quick as humanely possible...usually inside 30 days

Just go to www.inventionprep.com for instant access.

Go to www.inventionprep.com to learn how to start profiting off your idea in the next 30 days.

54

www.ingramcontent.com/pod-product-compliance
Lightning Source LLC
Chambersburg PA
CBHW071821170526
45167CB00003B/1393